OVER POUR

JANE WONG

ACTIONBOOKS
Notre Dame, Indiana 2016

Action Books
356 O'Shaughnessy Hall
Notre Dame, IN 46556

actionbooks.org

Joyelle McSweeney and Johannes Göransson, Editors

Zachary Anderson, Chris Muravez, Jeannie Yoon, 2016-2017 Editorial Assistants

Andrew Shuta, Book Design

Overpour © 2016 Jane Wong

Cover painting: Tessa Hulls, "Three Ways to Get the Carrot on the Stick," 2016

ISBN: 9780900575914
Library of Congress Control Number: 2016946065

Action Books is generously supported by the College of Arts and Letters
at the University of Notre Dame.

OVER POUR

Jane Wong

Contents

○

For my mother, Jin Ai, in awe

OVER
POUR

POEM

In the middle of the night

A cloud formed a storm inside my face

Garbage gathered in the storm

In the eye-ash

Nothing was wasted

The waste was covered over by ideas

At the very center of the storm

The sky was so blue you could hold it

In your hand and throw it like a bomb

For years I lived this way: with words

That had to do with carrion

I have learned to cast away my enemies

I have lit their insides clean

TWENTY-FOUR

Salt can dissolve
more – such is the law.

Antlers shine, bone
clean in our yard.

Buzzards at the bus stop
count off children.

We have two children.
To see how we truly behave,

we must lie side by
side and let anger slide.

This stupefied air
we hold a knife to,

to the neck. These nights,
crickets rave at the door.

Lamb's ear sprouts
a leprosy, softening

the yard. Our daughter covers
her mouth, smog

of the heart. Cloud and
cough, I couldn't even see

my hands in the morning.
The sky breaks open

how I break my roots
from you. Overpour

of regret, there is too
much blood in a cow

to comprehend.
At twenty, I halved caution

and called it Jane.
To want all that is

yours. I married you,
marred you, missed

your kill and kiss
for what? A continent away,

hay pours into a field.
Each time my father waves

across the shore, I dissolve
one part more.

AND THE PLACE WAS MATTER

and the branches shook the lights out
and the fish to be sold had their heads intact
and the highway expanded into four lanes
and the garlic blossomed in June
and this should not trouble us

•

What is there left to recover?
Dandelions weaved in my black hair
Too romantic, try again
I forgot to throw out the meat and the air stinks
Better
I tried to recover the air
I waved my arms around to gather a pile
The sky buckled at my jaw

•

I am afraid of trees that grow into themselves
The crows kicking at the root with their talons
Overgrowth of the organs, terrible
Branches rise from my mouth as if smoke could escape from a chimney
We have these frameworks, our skeletons, to keep us from getting tangled
Whenever I see a slug, I cover it with a leaf
It wears the leaf like a roof
These houses, trailing through the woods

•

and the cars piled atop each other
and the hospital added a wing
and the soup congealed in the refrigerator
and the garage opened manually

•

Once, I saw a wave unwork itself by buying out the moon
Investment in progress, in stars
In 1988, my mother modeled a sweater in a mail order catalog
My mother, in white, is exactly what winter should look like
I wrap myself in snow, in white, in my mother, and suddenly there is only
Ocean

•

Two arms crossed between two tables
My heart crossed between my eyes, out of focus
In January, I looked for winter underneath potted plants
But I found my brother instead
He had icicles for eyes
He was deep in the soil and made a home with slugs
They wrapped their bodies around his arms, overprotective
This is the way ignorance works: do not look under anything

•

and the grease lined the pan evenly
and the carnations were dipped in food color
and the onion grass covered the walkway
and the starfish dried out in the sun

•

Circular, my life is an endless nest
I have grown tired this way, carrying twigs in my mouth
Framework of my heart, bending
Did I consume the weaker bird?
You tell me

•

Sitting in a cave full of gems
The head can not focus
Light makes pyramids out of the body
Wouldn't it be nice to shine out like this?
To put myself in whoever's mouth and be exponential?
Light, light, little simplicity
I miss someone, but I don't know who

•

and my mother smiles in front of the camera
and the meat glistens in the plastic wrap
and my brother loses his skeleton
and the place was matter and all
and all but matter

DEBTS

Nothing is disturbed here
The mushrooms left to soak overnight

Have doubled
I am not ashamed to say

I ate them all
At once, my eyes shining with mold

To light my loathsome way

•

Was I paying attention?
The boiling potatoes barely kept the lid on

Overpour as if I could help it
This bath of spores, spoiled

In the boredom of six o' clock
My brother plays with his loose tooth

On the news, someone shoots his brother by accident
If I could drape guilt over me

Garlands of *I'm sorry for pushing you down the stairs*
Head to wall to head

It's enough to make your jaw hurt

•

I have fallen into a well again
This, I deserve

A caterpillar crawls onto my sleeve and stays there
This is all I have

Above, I can see
Someone setting off flares

Bright apples exploding
In the evening cool

•

My feelings are coming loose
I hear the stir of raccoons downstairs, all smudge faces

The raccoons sing around me, to-ing and fro-ing
Not exactly a refrain, but a clone to join

My brother has painted his face to become
Pure raccoon

•

Consider the rooms that outlast us
Consider the water left standing in a road

The flooded rice fields
Especially the crickets floating to the neck, singing:

There is a war in a country I have never heard of
There is a frontier in a country I have never heard of

•

Water dripped from the daffodils I pulled out
Of my brother's mouth

To speak in the voice of the Destroyer
I held my head under water and gurgled:

I have debts to pay
Wickedness clings to me

I have no choice
But to cling back

In the late afternoon
The lake shrugs off its leaves

Please do not watch
I had to cut open the slow-poaching sun

I had to

FAMILIAR STRANGER

To break a bottle,
you must fill it with chemicals
and calculate the pressure,
carefully. Had I spent all
day driving? It's hard to say.
A jacket falls out of a car
and it is my jacket,
half an arm dragging
on the road. Helpless chemical
embarrassment, tucked.
I kept the dirty hem of it,
my controlled leaving, leveled
out as a wall sound enough
to punch.

The radio detuned and
detonated, waveless.
A single note played,
splitting a horn
in half. I remembered:
I loved one as I
once had. The road sprawled
in front, my port of entry.
Hand over eye, I shielded
the steering sun,
as if looking at a noseless
marble statue, pure
indecency. I drove and drove,
Goddess of One Arm.

On a warm day,
a bottle expands, loses
its shape. Until certainty breaks
in half, I refuse
to move. The tulips here
are not for beauty
and thus must be killed.
We can't seem to forget the purpose,
the reason for it. Outside, the scaffolding
of a building leaves a marble
victory. I look into
my neighbor's window and see
myself, drawing a bath.
What could I have ever wanted?

Pine needles dry
in the sun. I cut a bone
lengthwise to show you
the marrow or there is everything
and nothing left. The fishmonger
wraps parchment over my fish
and this is my present.
A daughter throws an urn
into the sea, off Puget Sound.
The silver death mask
is the most difficult to accept.
Salt and brain, this fish.
The small heat of my arm nestles
among red pines.

Here, the chickens
are all garment, all feathers.
I grab one by the ankles
and take to the knives.
What is the distance
between reason
and beauty? I watered the plants
and they turned to plastic.
To take care of that
which we can not eat.
In the evening, a crab
disappears into the woods.
The mall opens its doors,
all anticipation.

It's 5AM,
my familiar stranger,
in the blinding wash
of a cauliflower sky.
Had I slept at the foot?
Raccoons wrestle in garbage
muck, piled at all
sides. I've tumbled into
nausea before and it was easy
to feel. This bad day
in my brain, washing out
as dirt washes out
from these mushrooms
I have de-stemmed.

The mall leaves its lights on:
my port of entry. Across town,
my grandmother carries
a head of lettuce
in a plastic bag, heavy.
Sliced in half,
I hold this rolling sound,
this heart, shaking off
its hinges. The woods run
along the crooked Taconic,
rattling in truck hollows.
This highway of us all.
Both of these hands, holding,
are mine.

PASTORAL POWER

You see: we have this idea of hunting each other.

The impact of the sun on your wrist is *first degree*.

The racket of birds and my knife is *second degree*.

Each blade of grass presses upon me as I rest too

long, spring and none. The nightly news runs

across my face, reads: the crime rate is *tenth degree*.

A heat wave sweeps over the Turnpike, sunflowers

fall along the Shrewsbury strip. In the car, my father

turns too fast and my mother slides across the seat,

window-face and all circumference. I am wrapped

in her sweater, a failing sight. Each signal I see

sees me: helicopters trailing through wool light.

Sometimes, I think: can Walden exist in China?

Returning to nature is a luxury we keep, like this

floral soap I can't bear to clean my filthy face with.

To leave the village, to return to the village in

a better dress. My cousin pissed out of a moving

van and there was sun, suffocating so. Sun

glimmering in the fish I eat down to the bones.

My life full of debt, indebted, in death do us.

My mother said the groundhogs ate all the eggplants.

And so she hit them with a shovel, one by one.

Little murders, little murders, peace unto you.

Fat spider of dread, spun up in half-eaten

crops. A good year, a bad year, another year.

To wash silk, you must wash it by hand or pay

someone to wash it for you. Red washes out

of an apple and the spell is broken. In Jersey,

the neighbor kid shows me a hole. "I'm digging

my way to China," he says. In winter, rabbits

nestle in the hole and freeze, ears first. I want

everything to spring up from the ground: grace,

forgiveness. I want the sun to stop following me,

to file a restraining order against the spiny beast.

Climb up on these shoulders of miniatures to see

the fallowing wilderness. Replicas of replicas and

the science fair kind. If I say the volcano will erupt

now, you better believe it. You better bail out

the sea, kill those geese in the parking lot and eat

them for dinner, dressed in rosemary and tar.

Five star meal, five stars in the night. Shining,

how I mistook a fountain in Vegas for my mother.

How I mistook Shenzhen for a forest of sneakers,

this economy in growth. I smiled from ear to ear,

glued in moss, the cheapest form of saccharine.

To those who owe and those who own us.

I might die paying off my loans if they don't

begin accepting dandelions. Defeat: pumice

trying to sink, 130 million migrants going

home for the new year. February, brace

your face for insults. My brother kicked

a raccoon out of the garage and cried for

days. Was it ever a question of sympathy?

In July, clusters of sun gather in secret

societies. The banks began charging for sleep.

A tourist spits into a hot spring on a breezy day.

A crane lifts a child out of a well and there is

no television crew. Clearly, discomfort makes

trees grow taller. With fertilizer, we can all shake

from the stems. My legs, dangling over the overpass.

Today, route 18 is all horns and heart. Under

a microscope, bacteria blooms readily, tiny mansions

of the self. Who am I to multiply? My grandfather

gathers chickens by the feet, wings flapping. If you

squint hard, he looks like a butterfly. In the near

future, I heard the continents will connect.

When we turn to each face other, it's a choice.

FIELD NOTES TOWARD WAR

The war is not over.
The streets are lined with little lamps of snow,

melting. Water pours without end.
There is a swan bathing in my mouth.

I have made a mess of it all.
Cotton in my eyes, too much

cast on my arm. All around me,
the mountains hum

a broth of air. A little on the tongue
is enough to feed. My eyes rinsed out

make a river large enough
to carry that which diminishes. I'm afraid

I will never make it home.

●

My mother feeds more envelopes during night shift.
The deer shift in limb light.

In the morning, we rake the yard.
She falls asleep in the yard, standing.

This bag of leaves, gathering.

•

Send death to swallow the war.
Send courage to tear each plume apart.

The sound of great wrestling.
It is enough to feed you.

•

The air settles like a magnet.
What choice do we have but to lean in?

The rocky regions of my brain quake.
It's one damn thing after another.

The mountain of granite has a face I recognize.
I drape a scarf across my eyes

and walk into every wall.

•

Eyes bloom along the cliffs.
The root of my brain recedes.

Together, my relatives carry the bodies.
I carry this bag of leaves into the garage.

Above me, the sun leeches.

THIRTY

Summer mold knits the Parkway,
headlights of velvet.

With what eyes can I see through
such bright confines?

My husband hits a tree at 55
and we spin a couple of lanes.

My eyes double over, as if in love
or at once lonely. We spin

and the insides of the car spill,
all sick in a marsh

of whiskey water. Cigarette ash
soothes Steven's wild teething.

He is awake and blinking to see
anything. Cars slow down

to watch us flail. All around us,
mosquitoes ignite small fires

and they are our fires.
A country away, I can hear oxen

snorting in milk-colored fog.
But in this country, in the small fires

of this spinning house,

the fingers of a highway fern

are brushing my lungs awake.

TWENTY-NINE

To live like a pill bug,
I curled into myself.

I greeted knee after knee.
Surely, it's too bad to want company.

To want this curling of my legs
around anyone's face.

These days, I have taken
to small boxes of self,

folded neatly for recycling.
These small towers at the ready.

To undo that which can't
be undone. At seventeen,

I cut a boy and hid in a barn
until the rice fields

rotted over. Spores of grain
inoculated the village.

In Jersey, forgiveness is an activity
too extracurricular

for the rose. In Jersey,
gulls dip their necks

into ice coolers. I press a can
against my cheek. Cold,

to watch some stranger
look and nothing more.

I imagine a queen surveying
her ruined empire centuries ago,

brick by thrown brick.
Each layer underfoot,

blood and rust and smoke.
I'm that person who can't stop

looking. I sweep the kitchen floor
with all the lights on.

I pry open every hill,
each ant with ribs of gold.

ELEGY FOR THE SELVES

What am I afraid of?
Everything flares up.

A star explodes,
traffic merges

into one lane.
The points of a star

nudge me in my sleep.
Wake up, weak lamp.

I come to, blink
in spots. A cloud offs

into a tree, a tree
sloughs off its leaves.

A leaf turns in the dark
and it is your back.

•

Death sits among
my things.

A dresser opens and
a mosquito flies out.

The sky above is full
of seeds, falling.

Each morning, watermelons
huddle in a market.

My grandfather bites
into a slice slowly.

The sun sloshes above.
A truck covers the sound

of the bite, the bite
covers the simmering sky,

the tired leaves on
the tired ground.

•

I carry these selves
everywhere.

How an ox carries
a family across

a flood, its bell
submerged and whistling

to and fro. I have
this habit of pouring

out just so. Water
in the dip of my roof,

mosquitos stretching
forth their legs,

thinned by wind
or thinned to waste

my crueler self.

•

Ants tunnel through
plum glow. Legs stuck

in heart, meat of
my sweeter self.

Twilight spreads a museum
of flies circling

my mother's wrist, a bracelet
of wings and eyes.

Too far to see, I threw
a horseshoe at no

particular stake
and it wrung

a neck. Fearless,
my little amp of a head,

resounding off.

•

Flour covers my face
and I laugh to be

a ghost. I let loneliness
slide through me,

kin to slug and
kind to no other.

I strike stone to stone
to make every fire

in every building.
This is self-love,

as we are taught.
The eye of an eel

my father turns on a spit,
rolling in my mouth.

It was summer
when I killed the first

self. The fire did
its work and left

nothing to see but
all to spark.

NO NEED FOR THE MOON TO SHINE IN IT

This life   in fits and starts: a spider walks across

the circumference of my room   with just one leg.

How easy we can adapt   if given one good thing:

one good leg, one good kettle, one   good patch

of grass.   In summer, I split the stems of a bouquet

to resemble legs kicking in a lake,   muddy all May.

In winter, we simply can't have   what we want.

I watch a fish freeze mid-flight in a waterfall.   Its eye:

a glassy rock I want to skip   into a pot

of soup to revive. February is fitting: my grandmother

yawns or shouts into her hands: salt-white   snow.

A cloak of bees covet   a fluorescent bulb, sunning

their wings. I stretch my legs across a rooftop. I am a line

of laundry drying, drawn in and   folded in

haste. My mother cuts small Xs   into tomato skins.

The tomatoes splinter in boiling water. My roiling heart:

pulped.   If I told you I felt safe all the time, I would

be lying. If I told you I lied,   I would also be lying.

A blush sweeps across my face like the sun in a smoke –

filled sky. False: trees are being set on fire.   False:

I used a broom to stir the bees up. True: the bees rained

down, singing dirges in every mouth   in every crown

in every sugar-rotten   cavity.

Under a full   moaning moon, I changed into a better

self: over-empathetic.   I saved every deer

tangled in every fence. I took hooves   to the face.

I won awards and gave awards away to terrible people so

they can feel something.   I adapted well

to dry climates. My leg hairs sprouted   like cacti.

How honorable, my eyes   impervious to tears, fire,

tectonic shifts of the self.   Look: I high-fived everyone

like a good citizen. I pinned every flag to every bone.

I burned garbage   to light the way for a family

of raccoons, crossing starless street after starless street.

Tell me: what kind of habits should I   adopt?

My braid dips   into the juices of a steak.

At 72, my grandmother's hair is so tangled we have to

shave her head. She is a little boy in a coat, three shades

too red. My grandmother says: there are so many ways

to be invisible. Salt-white   snow.

My heart softens: noodles in a pot.

A helicopter flying low can't mean good news,   no.

A weak cosmic ray transmits a message: give me all

your soft tissue, all your resilience. Go on: denude thyself.

Some cells split despite   death. When they opened

up the farmer, they found a grass clot   in his lungs.

I come from   a farming family. Which is to say,

I have killed plenty of things: spiders, ants, crabs –

leg by leg.   Murder is to mitosis is to mercy.

We are mostly legs too: part tendon, part pardon, kicking

or curling. My hair curls after falling into the ocean,

transverse wave of the face.   June never wavers:

I lick my arm for a pinch of salt. I pitch a fit and alternate

liking you.   Kiss me like this: all likelihood gambled:

how a dog barks to match the bark   of another.

Sorry does not mean   anything. Sore, though,

feels everything: my mother's arm feeding envelopes

into a machine, little workhorse of the heart and hoof.

So, lean against   me, I want to say. Take my

right hand, my right wrist –   it braces against

sorrow. I could row us away. My good arm, my good

daughter.   How easy we can adapt if given

something. Yesterday, I spent hours shucking corn,

the hairs of husks across my legs,   gathering.

All the animals that have committed to dirt have it all

figured out. A colony of ants is based on attachment:

everyone a bridge, everyone a   lean-to.

When I wake, I flail and startle   starlings. They topple

over, dropping insects out of their mouths.   This life:

shock, loss, shock. Would you turn away?   No need

for the moon to shine here.   No need for stop signs,

cold soups, laboratory goggles. Let your prized insects drop

from your mouth. Let the virus   hover over you,

knitting sickness like a thick winter scarf my mother wraps

around the both of us. Reroute   upon command.

Wash a plate like a fly washes its face. Eat an oyster without

opening it. Clean your good, bloody teeth.   Begin,

my mother, the conductor, says: begin, begin again.

BLOOD

My mother told me not to drink pig's blood
Unless I desire health
Gold should not enter the heart
Or be melted into teeth
But look how our faces shine
These crystallizing caves
Caved-in to keep
Our bloody splendor

•

Now you know where I've been
Black ink on palm, pumiced night
Face to face, we fought
In glory, in red, in arms our own
The soldiers filled the streets with shove and sea
Little stars, little flashlights in my hair
To clear myself from blame
I erased my birthmarks

•

Held under strong sunlight
Everything disappears or blooms
Peaches fall in the yard as we fall
Asleep, stunned and sweet
The saying goes and goes:
Keep your eyes closed when walking
Keep your close ones loved and close them

Walk hand in hand among the graves

•

To lead people into disaster
To boil a chicken with its head cut off
Why would someone do such a thing
One hundred flowers explode over our heads
I took shelter in stems and seed
I held your hand to make a root
To stay intact, we must keep everything in
No blood must be lost or stolen

•

If you bury something, do not pick it up
Chances are, it is a beast
It will bite you in the eye
Blindness will take your name
I do not know my grandfather's name
I know he cleaned soup bowls during the Cultural Revolution
I know to stay away from butterflies in butter, from counterfeit faces
To tell them apart

•

Can you tear yourself apart?
The leeches on my back have sprung open
A new organ grows in my heart
It is a double heart
Too much blood makes my eyes milk over
I am afraid to pour out and keep in

I wobble along the street
Everyone can see, everyone points

•

At home, my brother makes a habit of sleeping
Under transparent surfaces
Our kitchen table is made of glass and glistens
When he sleeps
I cough up a failure
In the middle of winter
My family huddles in the attic, dark lambs
The soap in my hair softens with snow

•

In summer, pig's blood swelters in a tin
A man kicks my mother
There is something wrong with his leg or she is in love
My mother cuts open his foot
She tells him: *where the sparks can not get through*
That's where you'll rest
My mother is seventeen and she cut a boy
I know her name is Jin Ai

•

A bone drops to the floor
Ants gather in corners, my family gathers their faces
This funeral of plenty
Sings dirges in the marrow
This living hand, now warm and capable
My blood thick with stars

ENCYCLOPEDIA, VOL.

What is it to begin in stillness?
No such thing. Remember how black
the ash trees shook in cloud light,
how easy it is to fear: honeycomb
in winter. At daybreak, shipyards are overrun
with buckets of fish. I could slip and fall through

The moss covered walls of a well

My mother draws a bath until it covers her knees.
A pot boils over and there is soup in my shoes.
Can we make this acceptable in any way?
Coal in the crocus plant, meat in the sink drain.
My father wraps a leather jacket around my brother's shoulders.
My brother crouches in a corner, small mountain of smoke

Confrontation of sky, the clouds are full of shoulders

The cause of grief is looking at a face.
The world is full of faces.
I can barely trust enough to clear a well-
worn forest. There is a clearing
in my throat large enough to build
a factory. Hundreds of women sitting
in a room with no windows.
Needlepoint swans, generous stitches
of red. The identical swaying of a ponytail I have tied
too tight to my crown. This is a habit
of mine. For certainty, I knock softly
at my fate. For grief, I listen with all my limbs

Slow organs, place your head against

A river only rises
in rain. A river only courses in one
direction. I don't know if this is true.
My father points to a store across the street and I walk toward it
with purpose. In a storm, the sky has purpose.
To glance below and say: what for? The land,
the animals, the people sitting in front of a television,
alone. This is the definition of sacrifice.
What is all this leaving good for? To return a face
we keep for keeping's sake? My mother laughs into a bowl of soup
or blows on it because it is too hot. The purpose of a spool of thread
is to calculate distance. My mother left home in 1982.
The hem of her wedding dress is 7,326 miles and what for

More cactus flower in your mouth

I am headed into fractured territory.
I run my hands through the sharp.
When I feel like something greater than myself,
I look backwards in a mirror, owl-
ready and growl like a newborn
rat. A hush releases into the air, the process
of becoming a force. I unwrap
a scarf from my neck, reveal

This immovable thing, the ocean has a face

A beetle vanishes from the ceiling. These days, I feel something
revolving around me. Magnet of the organs, my mother returns
the story to the beginning. She is a shadow that tries to latch
itself onto a surface. I am not afraid, I won't be
afraid. She sits me down on a chair. Watch, she says, pressing
a plum with the back of her hand, increasing pressure.
The planets rotate. I can not
help myself

To lose someone each day to everything is worse

Black coats sway in snow, bright
apples float in lake water. Stillness:
a new possibility. An unopened package of saltines
sits in my grandfather's vest pocket. I could crawl through

Among the dead trees, the blooming cabbage rose

All of Linnaeus's pupils died on their journeys.
Science is a process of discovery and documentation
of that discovery. My mother keeps her documents in a folder
under a pile of sweaters. Weather appropriate, science allows
enough progress to collide in the dark. This is where the question turns
its back to you. I let a man kiss me
in a chemistry lab. I stood naked in front of a chemical shower.
I knew I wasn't very old.
My eyes were as large as tidal pools

The green surface of water gathers insects, sticks, and birds

In a strong wind, I am at a loss.
To love a rock, one must carry it on their back.
For years, my mother caught moths in our
ceiling lamps, the wings grazing her cheek.
Sometimes, she stretches to touch
my neck. One tap and I am simply
halved

In the morning, there is an echo of singing in the air

THE ACT OF KILLING

It is early and I have no one to trust.

The sun wrestles wildly about me,

throwing light in unbearable places.

Each day, I wear this necklace of flares,

bright kicks against the throat. Each day,

the earth wobbles in its orbit. I am

in the process of creating an army.

A hive mind, honeyed in the eyes and

pure in purpose. Wasps drone among

roses I stole from my grandfather's

headstone. Drones watch as my father

kills a man over a bad bet. He presses

the man's head down into a floor flooded

with enough bills to build a country.

Covered in warm towels, my father drones

in his sleep. He sends a telegram to me:

I could have been a mathematician.

Equal signs multiply across state lines,

dividers of the familiar. Surveillance works

like this: stop. Intentions drag through

the mud, daily. The spoiled sun runs

its yolk. I run my mouth all over town.

All around me, the grievance tree weeps

with wasps. For, what is a bullet without

an arm to go through? I cross and cradle

my arms. When the sun goes down,

I check my eyes to see if they are still there.

FORTY-THREE

The buzz of a mosquito
warms my throat. Soon,

it will die; it is midnight
after all. I open the refrigerator

and scoop out the cheeks
of a fish. I call the fish

my husband. I call Jane
in Hong Kong but she doesn't

answer. I cut the ends off
a string bean and call

that Steven. These days,
there is dust on my forehead

I can't seem to dust off.
My cleanliness on loan,

the loans I owe stacked
neatly like bowls

of artichokes. To pry apart
my pride. Ice dissolves part

by part and is gone.
To not be able to call that

Myself. There is ozone

in the sky, gathering

the cruel words we say
to each other. I saw it

on TV, when I just
couldn't sleep.

GUTS

I enter a room.
A cat vomits as if to say

welcome home. Scattered
bones on the floor,

tiles of fur and fever:
welcome. Outside, the parks

are rinsed clean. Grass sprays
across my window.

This clean violence
for the Green and Livid.

•

Nothing I say leaves
this room. Not a foot,

not a single verb.
This room is meant

to be a cage to swing
sweetly in. Arm in

arm, slow scythe of
each doorway expanding

with each breath I hold in
until I can't.

Remember, what you can't
see can hurt you.

I will stay here,
getting fat in the eyes.

•

Braced against a wall,
I will bite at you.

I will take what
I've come to claim –

do not cry and
cry to no priest.

My mother told me
when consuming a whale,

take one bite at a time
or it will consume you.

Take heed. Take tail,
tongue, et al.

•

I enter the room
full of garlands slung

in a death march.
Flowers crowd the sill

in whiskey water.
I drink until my eyes

flood the entire state
of Jersey.

This year, there will be
a mudslide worth watching.

This year, we won't
need proof.

•

Outside, geese shit
on themselves.

It is the season of giving
and I gave everything

over to you: forgiveness,
apology, forgiveness.

Can you imagine roses
rotting in the trash?

It's simply too much.
Delicate February

and its dunce hat.

•

To pull a rabbit

out of what?

The future is not stupid.
To make a critical mass,

leave a spoon of honey
out for the ants.

This will be my army,
my kin. The yard

is lined with dumpsters
I know too well.

Sunshine spills
on the oil slick

of last night's dinner.
My face shines

in the slick, subtly
sublime.

•

In the case of a tornado,
retreat into the deepest

interior. Steal anything
you can get your hands on,

including yourself.
Nightly, my army

circles the earth's bruise.

Split plum of the heart,

stuck to the floor.
I'm unable to rightfully

stomp. Crows pass by
my pupils, recognizing

every face I shouldn't.
Decisions in confrontation.

Best to forgive or fork over
your better half.

•

The guts of a cow spill
onto the killing floor.

I scoop out the guts
of a cloud and smear it

across my eyes.
Intestinal, the false ray

of a false sun unravels.
I slither to the light,

suffocating so.
Below the horizon,

a crow flies across graves
off the interstate.

The pouring concrete

freezes, paralyzed

in ice, smog.

•

Sometimes, crickets go off
at the same time.

Sometimes, my legs itch involuntarily.
Sometimes, I want to be able

to hold my own hand.
This need is inhabitable:

fat tapeworm of the belly,
crooning in corridors.

TWENTY-FIVE

The trees here are poached
white. A peeled orange falls

from the kitchen counter,
a sweeter planet. Laughter fills

a honeycomb some distance
away. I give you a lie as cold

as a mirror in winter,
warm in fractals

of snow. No, I never did
say love. To alter and deny,

stand as still as any good
dead thing. Good possum,

good eagle splayed across
a windshield asking

for just enough forgiveness.
And who doles out

such charity? Yesterday, Jane
leaned against the stove

and burnt both her elbows.
To be responsible for

another life, I loathe it.
I did say loathe.

Upstairs, you sleep
with deadbolt eyes.

Downstairs, quick oats
bloat in the sink.

I throw a rake through
a pile of snow to feel

just enough violence.
In spring, the trees will rust.

CEREMONY

The cactus wants something more than water.
What have I left to give over to you?
Blossoms in the center spike.
It's hard to navigate streets I have forgotten on purpose.
My legs turn left each time, magnet of the Devil.
Lopsided leaves remind me to seek cover and covet.
In the middle of the night, the cat ate the heads off the flowers.
I almost killed her.
I imagined twisting the neck and confessed to no one.
I obsessed over the clean socket of a chicken wing.
Everyday hatred, everyday dread.
Stepping in water on the kitchen floor without expecting it.
Terrible, roots disengaging in overbearing light.
Terrible, the desert of our mouths, sweeping.

There are radioactive wolves in Chernobyl, flourishing.
This is all to say: anything is possible.
When we kiss, the smallest bones in my body amplify.
My eardrum mushrooms.
Kitchen grease blooms across my palm.
I hold onto a light bulb to become self-sufficient.
I lick a spoon to be closer to an inanimate object.
These actions, repeated, create a ceremony.
To test for failure, fall asleep in a doorway.
To worship havoc, kill something daily.
Terrible, to be banned from a funeral.
To watch a funeral across the street, in a car, with the windows rolled up.
My grandmother peels a grape as the coffin lowers.
Remember: do not look under anything.

A planet staggers forward, demanding attention.
The planet is not drunk, is not crying while kissing the back of your neck.
The back of your neck is not leaning into the kiss.
The rings are not Saturn.
Terrible, revolution in reverse.
Smoke bombs sit quietly in a field.
Mid-day, a deer startles me and I play dead.
My face, imprinted in green, is not a sight to be missed.
And how do I miss you if I do.
To test for resilience, swallow the pit of an avocado.
After dinner, apology sticks to my ribs.
I am in this eating contest, hollowing out my legs for you.
In Newfoundland, a blue whale is about to explode.
Rainbows of meat, as far as the eye can see.

A flower blooms in a parking lot, creating a field in need of water.
When the water comes, I pray to the falling and fall asleep.
I pare down the self – thin sliver of apple on the tongue.
For comfort, I slump into the soft concrete.
For cleanliness, ants and cigarettes wash my hair.
Vice has marked me with the footprints of ants.
The impassable stillness of the heart, pocked and pursed.
To swallow one's self whole, simply look in the mirror.
At the market, the mouths of herring hang open.
I touch my jaw, the ice counter, my temples, the counter.
My mother stuffs herring into a plastic bag and ties a knot.
At night, a rattlesnake wobbles out of a storm drain, ready to do my bidding.
I call to it as I call to you.
With a voice mixing flour and water for no reason whatsoever.

An architect folds a building inside of me.
The archways expand with each move.
Fax machines transmit documents each second of the day.
Exponential, the promise of capital in my arteries.
Investment in the ritual of breathing.
To keep steady, tell someone the truth at least once a day.
Such as: I grew so sick with worry, my heart leavened and filled an oven.
Such as: as much as I'd like to, I can not watch you die.
My lungs grow rooms upon rooms of lies.
Today, I laid down in trash heaps.
Heaps filled with soda lids, mistaken for tiny suns.
I beamed and basked in the sugar.
In 1968, my father nicked a goat's neck.
Nowadays, everyone can breathe easier.

A well fills with empathy, but no one falls in.
Instead, we put plagues on each other.
Fleas gather around our ankles, blood-jealous.
It's disheartening, to say the least, to plague yourself.
To wave to yourself in a mirror.
To say good morning amid a flora of fleas, singing.
In my defense, I have no limits.
Lines are drawn in no desert, in no wind.
Each morning, dust congregates on cheap wax tulips.
Each morning, my rattlesnake shakes itself out of the flour bin.
Ouroboros of the heart, hissing in clouds.
For knowledge, I kissed everyone and kissed them well.
I tiptoed to the edge of the well.
I threw a rock to see it swallow.

Giant tumbleweeds float across the movie screen like massive wigs.
I shake my hair to replicate such loneliness.
I count the days without another body to keep warm.
At the market, fish hang to dry, clothes-pinned by the tail.
I pin each promise to my lapel.
For empathy, trace the sloping sides of a highway waterpark.
For solitude, clean flour off a rolling pin.
Outside, a soiled mattress slumps on a street corner, completely free.
The moon will not make its debut tonight.
My rattlesnake has been swallowing a mouse for too many days.
I give him a heavy pour of salt to help the taste.
These days, I'm worried the earth will crease from too much stress.
These days, I wish I could tell you something.
Instead: the dangling legs of a horse trample me from above.

I hold a flashlight to your organs.
A liver should not be transparent.
I hold your liver like a dead, stinking shark.
I cradle your fins, your roving eye.
I cut slivers of my heart, onion-thin, good for any salad.
At night, mosquitos bite our eyes, bed bugs bite our thighs.
Flies beam from the compost and beckon us home.
Where do I bury the evidence of my failure?
For a better view, cut down a tree.
For mercy, share this roasted chicken.
The soap scum at the bottom of my tub grows another life.
This is what we were promised: another life.
Today, I run with a flare in my hand like a bouquet of exploding flowers.
Today, I will not be transparent.

THAW

The trees glowed in water

I had half an ice arm

I waved at the sun for warmth and connection

This melting chandelier of mine

A fever grew from my ankles up

A planet fell out of my mouth

My organs bloomed, parachutes in the night

Snowbells rang along my teeth

My verbs were all in disagreement

Swallowed up in the turbulence

In the rotten rumble of boiling eggs

I held the cold along the eyelashes of cows

I held my rosehip head, splitting in two

To remain perpetually aware

A feather suspended itself in air

The fish sitting too long in the sun melted

Into a sea, cell after cell

My prized imperatives, my root words: gone

Long live the day

Acknowledgments

Many thanks to the following journals in which these poems have appeared:

"Poem": *The Monarch Review*
"And the Place Was Matter" and "Debts": *The Volta*
Excerpts from "Familiar Stranger": *Hayden's Ferry Review, At Length,* and *The Wolf*
"Field Notes Toward War": *Salt Hill*
"Twenty-Nine" (as "To Live Like a Pill Bug"): *Pleiades*
"Elegy for the Selves": *The Laurel Review*
"No Need for the Moon to Shine in It": *The Margins (Asian American Writers' Workshop)*
"Blood": *Eleven Eleven*
"Thirty": *cream city review*
"Encyclopedia, Vol.": *The Seattle Review*
"The Act of Killing": *Tupelo Quarterly*
"Forty-Three": *The Pinch*
"Guts": *Pinwheel*
"Twenty-Five": *Newfound Journal*
Excerpts from "Ceremony": *Sixth Finch, Black Tongue Review,* and *cream city review*
"Thaw:" *Birdfeast*

"Pastoral Power" was made into a broadside by MIEL Books
"Twenty-Four" was made into a broadside by Poor Claudia Books
"Encyclopedia, Vol." appears in *Impossible Map,* a chapbook from Fact-Simile Editions
"Thaw" appears in *Best American Poetry 2015* (selected by Sherman Alexie) from Scribner

"Twenty-Four," "Twenty-Nine," "Thirty," "Forty-Three" and "Twenty-Five" are in my mother's voice, during that year of her life.

Grateful for: my mother, brother, and grandparents; my bright
stars and readers Hannah, Taryn, Nick, Ally, Melanie, Steve,
Michelle, Eddie, Sally, Cathy, and Diana; my beloved Kundiman
family and community; Joyelle, Johannes, and Don Mee at Action
Books for making this all happen; Tessa for her beautiful and wild
painting; my teachers, especially Mrs. L, Mat, Cole, Elizabeth,
and Brian; Bard College, the U.S. Fulbright Program, the Iowa
Writers' Workshop, the University of Washington, Hugo House,
and Mineral School for their writing support; my students who
keep engaging; Seattle, in moss and muck; Jersey, in sand and
trash; my family in China, a distance hard to grasp; and the ghosts
I hold close.